DANGEROUS DISEASES

Malaria

by Rebecca Pettiford

BLASTOFF! READERS, AN IMPRINT OF BELLWETHER MEDIA BY FLUTTERBEE

Blastoff! Readers are carefully developed by literacy experts to build reading stamina and move students toward fluency by combining standards-based content with developmentally appropriate text.

Level 1 provides the most support through repetition of high-frequency words, light text, predictable sentence patterns, and strong visual support.

Level 2 offers early readers a bit more challenge through varied sentences, increased text load, and text-supportive special features.

Level 3 advances early-fluent readers toward fluency through increased text load, less reliance on photos, advancing concepts, longer sentences, and more complex special features.

★ **Blastoff! Universe**

Reading Level

Blastoff! Beginners — Grade K

Blastoff! Readers — Grades 1–3

Blastoff! Discovery — Grade 4

This edition first published in 2027 by Bellwether Media, Inc.

For information regarding permission, write to Bellwether Media, Inc., Attention: Permissions Department, 3500 American Blvd W, Suite 150, Bloomington, MN 55431.

Library of Congress Cataloging-in-Publication Data is available at www.loc.gov or upon request from the publisher.

ISBN: 9798898800666 (hardcover)
ISBN: 9798898801908 (ebook)

Editor: Suzane Nguyen Designer: Brittany McIntosh

Printed in the United States of America, North Mankato, MN.

Table of Contents

What Is Malaria?

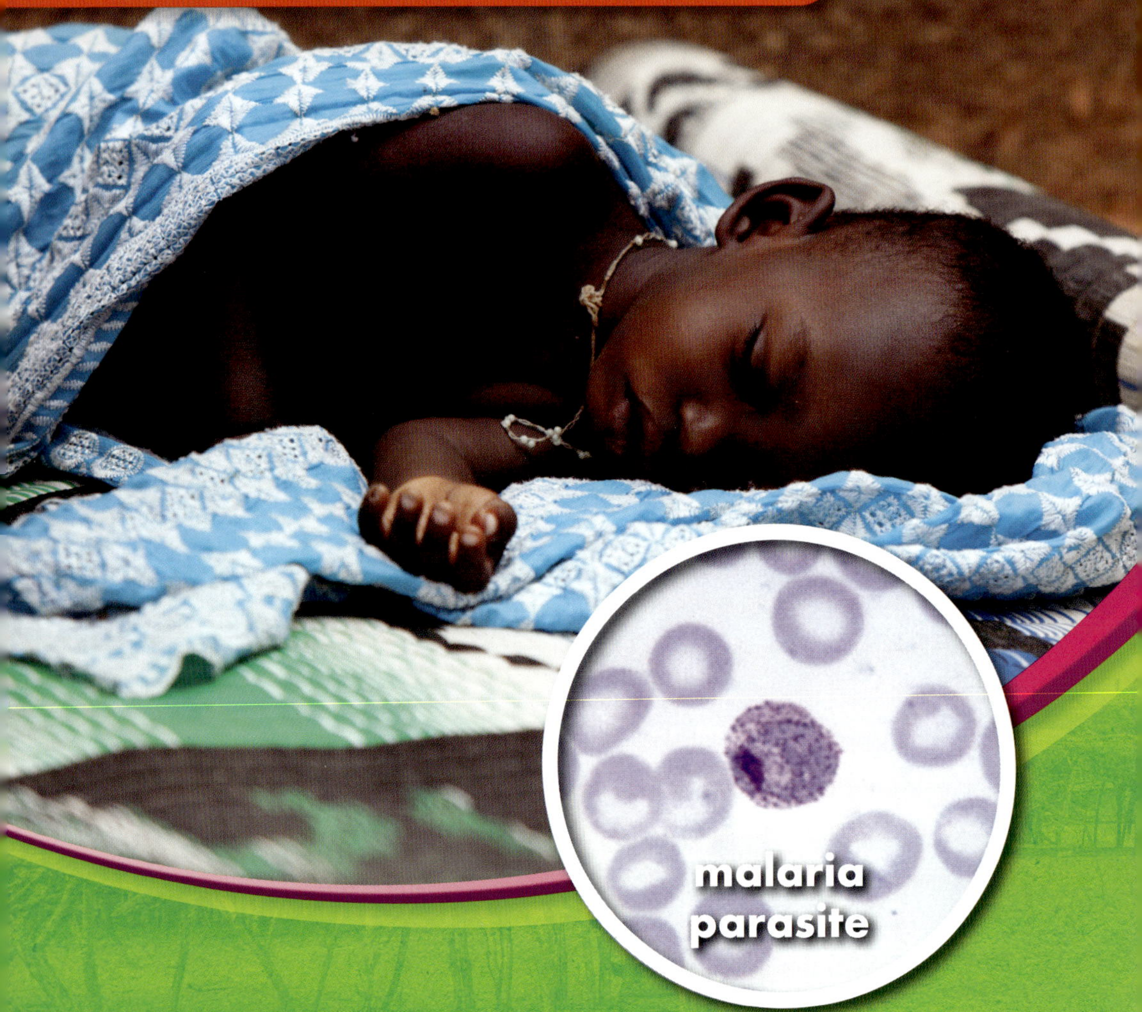

malaria parasite

Malaria is an illness caused by a **parasite**. The parasite is found in some female mosquitoes.

Malaria spreads when people are bitten by **infected** mosquitoes.

Almost 300 million people get malaria every year. Around 600,000 people die from it each year.

It Started with Gorillas

Malaria started in gorillas. At some point, the parasite jumped from gorillas to humans!

Signs include a high **fever** and chills. People can have breathing problems. Some people get yellow skin!

History of Malaria

Malaria is common in **tropical** parts of Africa and Asia. It has been around for thousands of years. **Ancient** people even wrote about it!

For a long time, no one knew how it spread.

French doctor, Charles Louis Alphones Laveran

In 1880, a French doctor found the parasite that causes malaria.

Timeline

1880

Doctor Charles Louis Alphones Laveran finds the parasite that causes malaria

1897

Doctor Ronald Ross shows that mosquitoes carry malaria

1971

Tu Youyou makes a medicine that treats malaria

In 1897, an English doctor learned that mosquitoes carried the illness. In 1971, a Chinese scientist made **medicine** to treat it.

How Does Malaria Spread?

A female mosquito bites someone with malaria. It gets the parasite.

The parasite stays in the mosquito. The mosquito bites a healthy person. The parasite is in its **saliva**. The person gets sick.

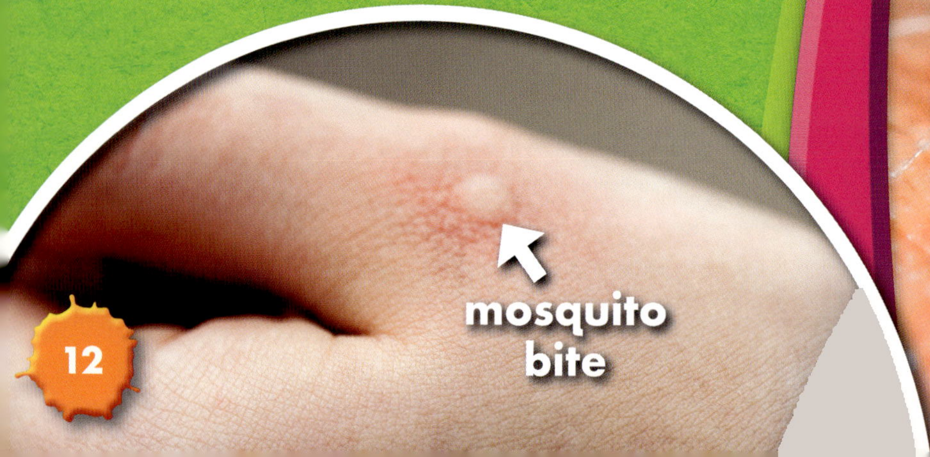

How Malaria Spreads

1

A mosquito bites someone with malaria.

2

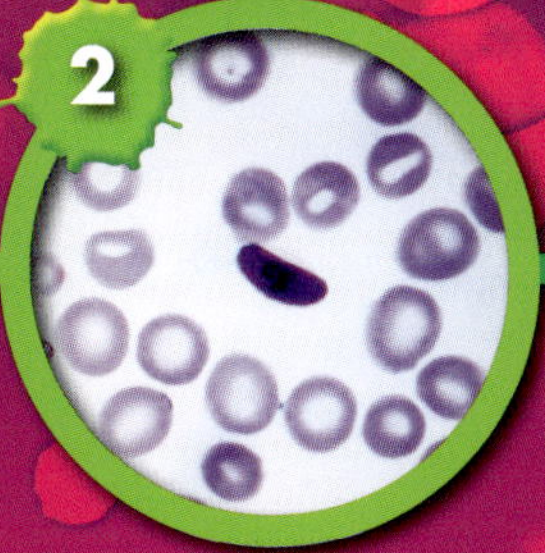

The mosquito carries the malaria parasite.

3

The mosquito bites a heathy person and they get sick.

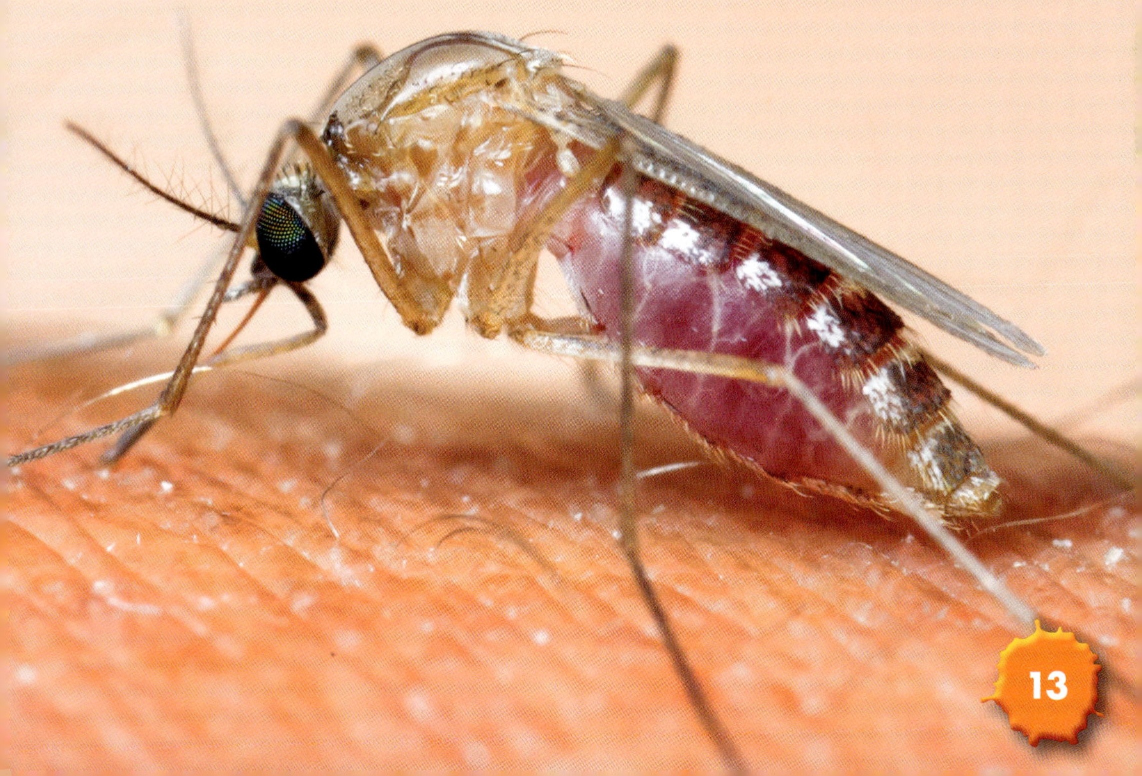

Travelers and pregnant women have a high risk of getting malaria.

Many people who die from the illness are children. They are not yet strong enough to fight the illness.

Prevention and Treatment

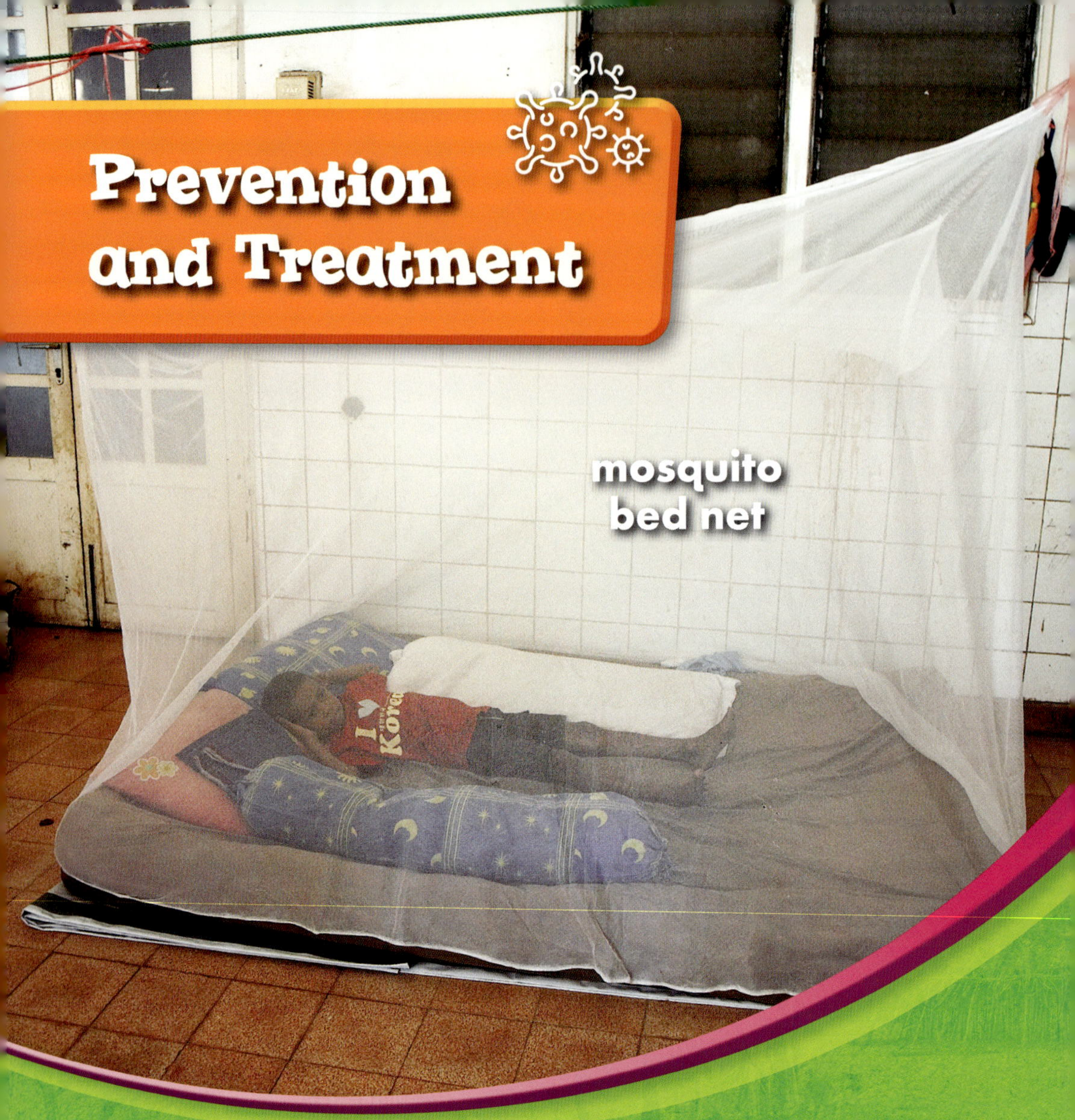

People use bug spray. It helps keep mosquitoes away. They also use bed nets for sleeping.

It is getting harder to kill mosquitoes. Many are **resistant** to bug sprays.

If people get sick, it usually takes up to 30 days for signs to show.

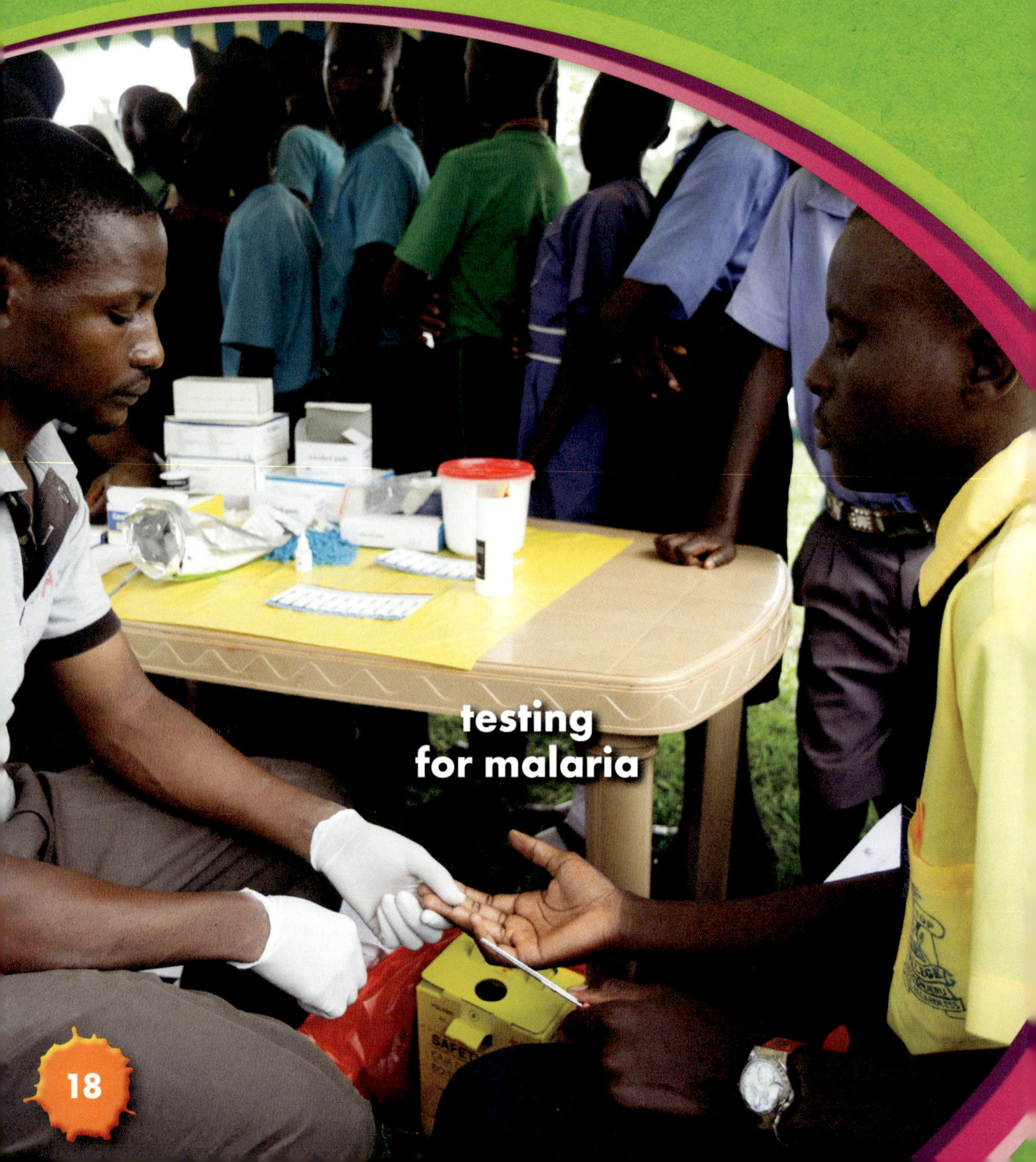

testing for malaria

Healing Hero

Name

Tu Youyou

Year Helped

1971

How She Helped

Tu Youyou made a drug that treats malaria. She won a Nobel Prize for her work!

There are medicines that treat malaria. They kill the parasites! If found early, malaria can be treated fast.

It takes up to 14 days to treat malaria. Malaria is often **fatal** if not treated right away.

There is a **vaccine**. It is given to young children. It helps fight malaria!

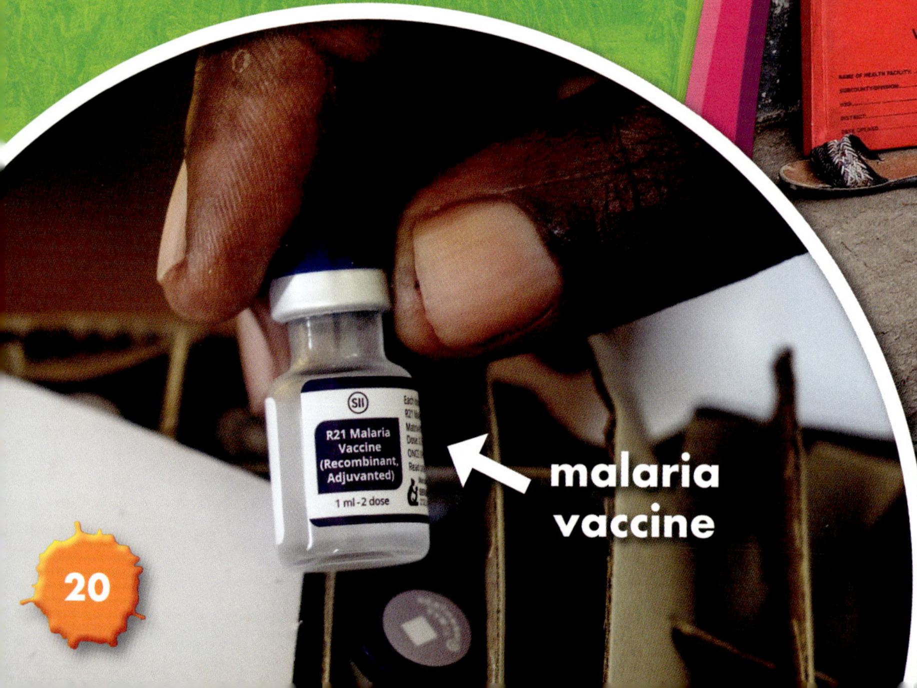

malaria vaccine

THE ONE

Glossary

ancient—from long ago

fatal—causing death

fever—a higher-than-normal body temperature

infected—impacted by a harmful illness

medicine—something taken to treat an illness

parasite—a small living thing that lives in or on another living thing and feeds from it

resistant—not harmed by something

saliva—a liquid that is made in the mouth to break down food

tropical—having to do with a place that is hot and wet

vaccine—a substance that is put into the blood to help fight off an illness; a person who has gotten the vaccine is vaccinated.

To Learn More

AT THE LIBRARY

Bates, Mary. *Malaria.* Minneapolis, Minn.: Abdo Publishing, 2022.

Kukla, Lauren. *I'm a Doctor.* Rochester, Minn.: Mayo Clinic Press Kids, 2024.

Pattison, Darcy. *Fever: How Tu Youyou Adapted Traditional Chinese Medicine to Find a Cure for Malaria.* Little Rock, Ark.: Mims House, 2022.

ON THE WEB

FACTSURFER

Factsurfer.com gives you a safe, fun way to find more information.

1. Go to www.factsurfer.com.
2. Enter "malaria" into the search box and click 🔍.
3. Select your book cover to see a list of related content.

Index

The images in this book are reproduced through the courtesy of: Kletr, front cover (hero), p. 3; James Gathany, Dr. Frank Collins, University of Notre Dame, USCDCP/ Wikipedia, front cover (splatter top), p. 5; MaryBeth Semosky, front cover (splatter bottom); Artush, front cover (background); Irene Abdou/ Alamy Stock Photo, p. 4; CDC/ Steven Glenn, Laboratory & Consultation Division/ Wikipedia, p. 4 (inset); Richard Juilliart, p. 6; Hung Chung Chih, p. 7; Iryna Shpulak, p. 8; Friedrich Stark/ Alamy Stock Photo, p. 9; Tunatura, pp. 10-11; World History Archive/ Alamy Stock Photo, p. 10 (inset); Photo 12/ Alamy Stock Photo, p. 11; Vaida.abd, p. 12; 7th Son Studio, pp. 12-13; James Gathany/ Wikipedia, p. 13 (step 1); CDC/ Dr. Mae Melvin/ Wikipedia, p. 13 (step 2); Павлик Лисицын/ Wikipedia, p. 13 (step 3); ALEXANDER BEE/ Alamy Stock Photo, p. 14; Carlos Duarte, p. 15; Sean Sprague/ Alamy Stock Photo, p. 16; SeventyFour, p. 17; Adam Jan Figel, p. 18; WENN Rights Ltd/ Alamy Stock Photo, p. 19; Hajarah Nalwadda/ Stringer/ Getty Images, pp. 20, 20-21.